Read It! Draw It! Solve It!

PROBLEM SOLVING FOR PRIMARY GRADES
TEACHER RESOURCE BOOK

Elizabeth D. Miller

GRADE TWO

Dale Seymour Publications®

Managing Editor: Catherine Anderson
Product Manager: Lois Fowkes
Senior Editor: Jeri Hayes
Project Editor: Julie Carlson
Production/Manufacturing Director: Janet Yearian
Senior Production Coordinator: Alan Noyes
Design Manager: Jeff Kelly
Cover Design: Alison Jewett-Furlo / Square Moon Productions
Cover Illustration: Stan Tusan / Square Moon Productions
Text Design: Square Moon Productions

Dale Seymour Publications® is an imprint of Addison Wesley Longman, Inc.

This Book Is Printed
On Recycled Paper

ISBN 1-57232-435-X
Order number DS33801

6 7 8 9 10 -ML- 01 00

Why This Program Was Created

Read It! Draw It! Solve It! is a unique problem-solving program designed for children from reading readiness through third grade. It was created to increase young children's understanding of mathematical concepts through direct visual involvement. For each problem in the program, students will demonstrate their understanding of the concept by creating a drawing before providing the answer.

Students who use this program become confident in their reasoning abilities and are able to communicate easily their understanding of mathematics. When young children work with illustrations they have made rather than abstract symbols, they learn to think of mathematics as problem solving rather than rote learning. They learn to reason rather than simply react, and they develop a better understanding of what they are doing. They also learn to read carefully because they know that they will have to demonstrate their understanding with a drawing.

Students love the open-endedness of the problems. The program encourages creativity in thought and expression, and it celebrates diversity. No two drawings will ever be the same, and many of the problems lend themselves to a variety of solutions.

Moreover, when students illustrate problems, the teacher gets a better understanding of their thought processes. If an answer is incorrect, it is usually easy to tell from the child's drawing where the student went wrong. Given the problem, "Nine people have come to the dance. Can everyone have a partner?" one boy made a picture of nine happy people in a row and answered "Yes." He had read the question as, "Can everyone have a party?" When his teacher helped him to read the problem correctly, he altered his illustration and answered "no."

How to Use This Book

Each book contains 180 problems, one for each day of the school year. The routine is the same throughout the program, although at the beginning of the year you will want to be sure to follow the activity with a discussion period to be sure any questions are answered fully.

Your task is simply to distribute the daily problem to the class and read it aloud if necessary. Students decide on the essential elements, make appropriate illustrations, and only then go on to provide solutions. Be sure they know that they are to draw the picture *first*.

Samples of Student Work

by Lauryn Draessler

Henry can juggle 12 oranges at once. He is holding 4 of them in his hands.

How many oranges are in the air? _____ 8 _____

If they give him 18 oranges, how many of them will land on the floor?

_____ 6 _____

by Evan Daniel

We are playing hockey. The blue team has 10 people. The red team has 8 people.

How can we make the teams equal? _take away 2 from the blue_

_team_____

The chart below lists the math concepts that appear on second-grade mastery tests, with the pages in this book that provide practice problems for those concepts.

MATH CONCEPTS FOR SECOND GRADE MASTERY	PAGES WITH PRACTICE PROBLEMS
patterns	3, 11, 31, 49, 55, 129, 130, 176
regrouping	103, 106, 107, 108, 109, 110, 111, 112
fractions	17, 24, 29, 40, 47, 52, 150, 151, 152, 154, 155, 157 158, 159, 162
multiplication and division	14, 15, 18, 19, 20, 21, 23, 27, 30, 33, 34, 35, 38, 44, 53, 54, 56, 58, 67, 68, 72, 76, 78, 86, 87, 90, 127, 128, 132, 134, 142, 144, 146, 147, 148, 156, 165, 167, 168, 169, 174, 175
addition and subtraction	1, 28, 37, 43, 45, 46, 48, 60, 71, 73, 77, 88, 119, 133, 135, 139, 160, 161, 177, 179, 180
more/less	4, 5, 7, 8, 9, 10, 12, 26, 42, 57, 59, 74, 81, 101
attributes	121, 122, 123, 124, 125
graphs, charts	143, 145
write problems	61, 62, 63, 64, 65, 66, 80, 82, 83, 84, 85, 113, 114, 115, 116, 117, 118
time	137, 138, 140, 141, 153, 163, 164
measurement	36, 50, 91, 92, 93, 94, 95, 96, 97, 98, 99, 100, 136, 166, 170, 173
money	25, 39, 89, 126, 131, 171
shapes	70, 79, 120, 149, 178
equivalence	2, 6, 13, 16, 22, 32, 33, 41, 51, 69
#s to 100	75, 102, 104, 105

You may want to use this program as it was set up—one problem a day—or you may want to pick and choose problems according to the needs of your students and how they fit into your other curriculum areas. Note, however, that the problems increase in reading and mathematical difficulty over the course of the year.

Learning To Think Through Reading And Math can be integrated with any math or reading program. Blank templates are provided for you to make up special problems for your class that incorporate specific information your students are learning.

Also offered in this set is an animal themes program with 45 problems each for kindergarten through third grade. These exercises require students to demonstrate understanding of animal attributes as well as math concepts, and provide an intriguing supplement to animal studies units that you may be doing at any of these grade levels.

What Your Students Will Learn

The overall format for the second grade is similar to that for the first-grade level. Each student will receive a daily problem to illustrate and solve. In second grade we use numbers from one to one hundred, and many problems have two steps. Vocabulary is more difficult than at the first-grade level, and students use their reading and writing abilities to demonstrate understanding of the following mathematical concepts:

- patterning
- addition, subtraction, multiplication, and division of whole numbers to 18
- grouping according to attributes
- fractions
- simple geometric shapes
- measurement
- writing story problems from number sentences
- solving problems involving order and magnitude of whole numbers

The second- and third-grade programs belong in the third, or "reading comprehension" stage of reading instruction. Some students, however, may not be able to read and may not understand how to proceed. Read the problem aloud and discuss it before asking students to make illustrations.

The first problem in second grade is a simple one.

> Here are nine cats. Six cats are black. The rest are yellow. How many yellow cats are there?

Problems increase in complexity as the year progresses. On day 14 we present the two-step problem:

> Patrick has a hard time getting his work done. His teacher agreed to give him three stickers every time he completes a paper. Patrick has completed three papers today.
>
> How many stickers must his teacher give him? _____
> If he completes five papers, how many stickers must she give him? _____

Make sure that they read all of the problem and answer both questions.

Facility with reading increases rapidly during the second grade year. Some problems, however, contain words that students can read but will not fully understand. The teacher must be aware of this potential problem and be prepared to explain the vocabulary. On day 161 we have the problem:

In our garden we have five tulips.
We have four times as many daisies as tulips.
We have half as many daffodils as daisies.

How many daisies? _____
How many daffodils? _____

In this case, the teacher will need to explain to some students what *four times as many*, and *half as many* mean.

Problem #178 presents a word that students may not have encountered before.

Draw a design with one circle, one square,
one rectangle, and one triangle.
Make the design symmetrical.

Explanation of the word *symmetrical* should be a whole group activity. It might be a good idea to also discuss the word *design* at this time.

Analyzing delightful illustrations is a lot more fun for a teacher than simply correcting papers. More important, the analysis helps the teacher to better understand individual thought processes, and then to provide appropriate encouragement and assistance. The better a teacher understands each student, the higher will be student success rate.

Instead of "training" students in specific strategies, this program educates young people to discover what it takes to solve any kind of problem. Because of this approach, students are not intimidated when confronted with novel situations. They learn to look for more than one way to solve a problem—and sometimes for more than one answer. Perhaps the most exciting aspect of this program is that as students develop confidence in their reasoning abilities they take this confidence with them into other areas of the curriculum.

Blank Template

Use the template that follows to provide your students with special problems that pertain to the work they are doing.

Here are nine cats. Six cats are black. The rest are yellow.

How many yellow cats are there? _____

The green volleyball team has four girls and two boys.
The blue team has five boys.

How many girls does the blue team

need to make the two teams equal? _____

+---+
| |
| |
| |
| |
| |
| |
| |
| |
| |
| |
+---+

Eleven students are lined up at the drinking fountain.
Every other student is a boy.
The first, third, fifth, and seventh students are boys.

Which other ones are boys? _____

_____

(blank box)

At my farm we have two cows, one horse, three chickens,
and four sheep.

Is the number of sheep greater than the number of pigs? _____

Are there fewer horses than chickens? _____

Are there more chickens than cows? _____

┌───┐
│   │
│   │
│   │
│   │
│   │
│   │
│   │
│   │
│   │
│   │
│   │
│   │
└───┘

The children are building block towers. They want to see who can build the highest one. The blocks are all the same size. Carl has stacked up three red blocks, four yellow ones, and two blue ones. Betsy has four red ones, five yellow ones, and one blue one. Maria doesn't have any red ones, but she has seven yellow ones and one blue one.

Who has the tallest stack? _____

Who has the shortest? _____

Nari's toy shelf has six dolls on it. Juan's toy shelf has eight dolls on it. We want Nari and Juan to have the same number of dolls.

How can we do it?

_____

_____

_____

[blank box for drawing]

Elena is selling turtles. She started with ten turtles.
She sold three to Raul, two to David, and four to
Amalia.

How many turtles are left? _____

Who has the most turtles? _____

Who has the least? _____

Silvia has ten marbles in a row. The first, third, fifth, and seventh marbles are red. The rest of the marbles are blue.

Which marbles are blue? _____

Are there more red marbles than blue? _____

Our pals are coming for lunch. We have four plates
of sandwiches. The blue plate has four peanut
butter sandwiches and two ham sandwiches.
The red plate has seven peanut butter sandwiches.
The yellow plate has two peanut butter sandwiches
and seven ham sandwiches. The green plate has two
peanut butter sandwiches and six ham sandwiches.

Which plate has the most sandwiches? _____

Which plate has the fewest sandwiches? _____

Which sandwiches do we have more of,

peanut butter or ham? _____

A touchdown is worth six points. A field goal is worth three points.

In the first game my team made two touchdowns.
In the second game we made five field goals.
In the third game we made one touchdown and three field goals.
In the fourth game we made two touchdowns and one field goal.

Make a chart to show this.

In which game did we make the most points? _____

In which game did we make the least points? _____

Make a row of numbers 1 to 10.

Above each even number, draw a picture of something sweet to eat.

Above each odd number, draw a picture of something to eat that is not sweet.

```
┌─────────────────────────────────────────────┐
│                                               │
│                                               │
│                                               │
│                                               │
│                                               │
│                                               │
│                                               │
│                                               │
│                                               │
│                                               │
│                                               │
└─────────────────────────────────────────────┘
```

Jan has 3 bananas and 4 apples. Peg has
1 more banana and 2 fewer apples than Jan has.
Ed has 2 fewer bananas and 1 more apple than
Peg has.

Who has the most fruit? _____

Who has the least fruit? _____

Tyrone and Alberto traded baseball cards for marbles.
They decided that each card was worth three marbles.
Tyrone gave Alberto six baseball cards.

How many marbles must Alberto give to Tyrone? _____

How many baseball cards could Alberto get for 24 marbles? _____

┌───┐
│   │
│   │
│   │
│   │
│   │
│   │
│   │
│   │
│   │
│   │
└───┘

Patrick has a hard time getting his work done. His teacher agreed to give him three stickers every time he completes a paper. Patrick has completed three papers today.

How many stickers must his teacher give him? _____

If he completes five papers,

how many stickers must she give him? _____

It is raining at the beach. Everyone is sitting under an umbrella.
Four people are sitting under each umbrella. There are four umbrellas.

How many people are at the beach? _____

If five people were sitting under each umbrella,

how many people would there be? _____

There are six boys and four girls on the green team.
There are five boys and seven girls on the blue team.

How can we make the teams equal? _____

_____

_____

I divided a melon in half. Then I cut each half into
equal pieces. I gave the pieces from one half to Shari,
Victor, Susana, and José. Each of them got one piece.

How many pieces are left? _____

How many pieces were there before I gave some away? _____

Four black swans are swimming on the lake. Twice as many white swans are swimming on the lake.

How many white swans are there? _____

How many swans in all? _____

Seven children are sipping milkshakes. Each child
has two straws.

How many straws? _____

If each child had three straws,

how many straws would there be? _____

Four lions are lying on their backs with their paws up in the air.

How many paws do we see? _____

How many ears? _____

My group has four people in it.

Rachel's group has double that number.

How many people are in Rachel's group? _____

We are going to plant flowers.

How many shovels do we need? _____

How many gloves? _____

The purple team has six boys and eight girls.
The orange team has seven boys.

How many girls does the orange team

need to make it equal to the purple team? _____

Each player has a flag. How many flags do we need? _____

A starfish has five arms. There are five starfish on the beach.

How many arms are there on the beach? _____

How many arms would there be if there were six starfish? _____

Mom served apple pie. John ate $\frac{1}{2}$ of the pie.

Thomas ate $\frac{1}{4}$ of the pie.

How much of the pie was eaten? _____

How much of the pie is left? _____

Manuel has 2 dimes, a nickel, and a penny.
Brenda has 1 dime, 2 nickels and 10 pennies.
Charley has 3 dimes, 1 nickel, and 0 pennies.

Who has the most money? _____

Who has the least money? _____

If we put all the money together,
how much money would there be? _____

_____

Ricardo, Edward, and Sanjay are building stone walls.
Ricardo's wall is 4 rows high with 5 stones in each row.
Edward's wall is 3 rows high with 7 stones in each row.
Sanjay's wall is 2 rows high with 9 stones in each row.

Who has the most stones? _____

Who has the fewest stones? _____

How many stones have been used? _____

Five sailboats are racing on the lake. Each sailboat has two sails.

How many sails in all? _____

Each boat lowered one sail. Now how many sails are up? _____

I have 4 red cups, 5 blue cups, and 6 green cups.
I have 9 saucers.

How many more green cups than red cups do I have? _____

How many more saucers do I need

to have a saucer for each cup? _____

George's math paper has 12 problems. He got 6 of them right.

How many did he get wrong? _____

George divided his paper into 4 equal parts.

How many problems were in each part? _____

Ten rabbits are riding in wagons. Two rabbits sit in each wagon.

How many wagons are there? _____

Three jump out of the wagons. How many rabbits are

still riding in wagons? _____

Make a row of numbers 1 to 12. Above each even
number, draw a shape using straight lines. Above
each odd number, draw a shape using curved lines.

Starting with the first one, color every third shape red.

How many red shapes with straight lines are there? _____

Name _____

We are playing hockey. The blue team has ten people.
The red team has eight people.

How can we make the teams equal? _____

_____

_____

_____

There are 28 pears growing on 4 trees.
There are the same number of pears on each tree.

How many pears on each tree? _____

If Jomel picks 10 pears, how many pears

will be left on the trees? _____

There are 30 apples growing on trees in the orchard.
Each tree has 6 apples.

How many trees are there? _____

If there were 30 apples, but only 5 apples on each tree,

how many trees would there be? _____

(blank box)

Six children are roasting marshmallows. Each child has five marshmallows on a stick.

How many marshmallows are there? _____

How many marshmallows will there be

when each child eats two? _____

Main Street can hold four houses. About how big would one house be? Make a picture of it in the box.

Main Street

If Main Street could only hold three houses, about how big would one house be?

Main Street

We have four brown cows and three black ones.
Each brown cow has one calf.
Each black cow has two calves.

How many calves? _____

How many animals in all? _____

[blank drawing box]

Our desert island has 6 palm trees. Each tree has 4 leaves.

How many leaves? _____

There are 2 coconuts in each tree.

How many coconuts? _____

The bakery sells bread for 10 cents and bagels for 5 cents.
I have 30 cents.

What can I buy?

_____

_____

_____

_____

We divided a pizza into 12 equal slices. Each of us got 3 slices.
We ate the whole pizza.

How many of us are there? _____

If there were two of us, how many

slices would each of us get? _____

[blank drawing box]

Red blocks are twice as heavy as blue blocks.
We have three red blocks on one side of the seesaw.

How many blue blocks do we need to put on the

other side of the seesaw to make it balance? _____

If we put four blue blocks on one side, how many

red blocks would we need on the other side? _____

READ IT! DRAW IT SOLVE IT! • GRADE 2

41

(blank box)

Irene read 6 books on Tuesday, 3 on Thursday, and 5 on Saturday. James read 2 books on Monday, 7 on Wednesday, and 4 on Friday. Carmen read 4 books on Monday, 5 on Thursday, 2 on Friday, and 1 on Saturday.

Who read the most books? _____

Who read the fewest books? _____

On which day were the most books read? _____

□

There are 11 players on a football team. Two teams are on the field. We have 18 helmets.

How many more helmets do we need? _____

How many shirts will we need? _____

How many shoes? _____

Three rowboats are on the lake. One octopus sits in each rowboat.

How many tentacles all together? _____

If each octopus is using four oars,

how many oars are there? _____


```
┌─────────────────────────────────────┐
│                                     │
│                                     │
│                                     │
│                                     │
│                                     │
│                                     │
│                                     │
│                                     │
│                                     │
└─────────────────────────────────────┘
```

Five of us went to pick watermelons. Anne picked two, Tani picked eight, Benjamin picked four, Rosa picked three, and I picked five. Each of us could carry only two watermelons to the car in one trip.

Who only had to make one trip? _____

How many trips did Benjamin have to make? _____

How many trips did Tani have to make? _____

[blank box]

I had to do two math papers on Monday. On Wednesday
I had to do twice as many. On Friday I had to do twice as
many papers as I had to do on Wednesday. On Thursday I
did one more paper than I did on Monday, and on Tuesday
I did one more paper than I did on Thursday.

How many papers did I have to do on Tuesday? _____

How many papers did I have to do on Wednesday? _____

How many papers did I have to do on Thursday? _____

How many papers did I have to do on Friday? _____

[blank box]

We are saving pennies to buy a treat for the class.
Sofia has ten pennies.
Kwan has twice as many pennies as Sofia.
Tim has half as many pennies as Sofia has.
Yi-min has half as many pennies as Kwan has.
Lilla has twice as many pennies as Tim and Yi-min have together.

How many pennies do we have? _____

The teacher wants us to read 20 books by the end of the year.
Arthur has read 18. Nita has read 4. Carlos has read 12.
Yoshi has read 9, and Eduardo has read 15.

How many more books does each student have to read?

Arthur _____

Nita _____

Carlos _____

Yoshi _____

Eduardo _____

Make a row of numbers, 1 to 4.

Above the odd numbers, draw a picture of a kind of transportation that has an engine.

Above the even numbers, draw a picture of a kind of transportation that does not have an engine.

Make pictures of what you might use to measure these things:

a football field

milk for cooking

time

a piece of paper

There should be 6 players on each team.

If there are 24 people in the class,

how many teams can we have? _____

If there are 19 people in the class,

can everyone be on a team? _____

How many extra people will you have? _____

What happens if there are 26 people in the class? _____

_____

Make a square and divide it into quarters.

Color $\frac{1}{4}$ red and $\frac{3}{4}$ blue.

If you made four squares like that one,

how many red spaces would

you have? _____

How many blue spaces would you have? _____

Our barn holds 5 cows.

How many barns of the same size

would we need for 20 cows? _____

How many barns would we need for 40 cows? _____

There are ten pairs of dancers on the dance floor.

How many people are dancing? _____

When five more couples come,

how many people will there be? _____

[blank framed box]

The blue team got the odd numbers starting with 1.
The red team has even numbers starting with 2.
There are 12 people on each team.

What is the highest number? _____

Which team has the highest number? _____

If the highest number were 26, could the teams be equal? _____

If the highest number were 29, could the teams be equal? _____

There are 14 girls and 12 boys at the class party.

How many smiles? _____

How many shoes? _____

[blank box]

There are four houses on our street. Ben lives with his mother,
grandmother, and two sisters. Sasha lives with her mother,
father, and three brothers. Andy lives with his aunt, his uncle,
and his grandfather. Pete is one of a set of quintuplets.
They live with their mother, father, and one older sister.

Whose house has the most people in it? _____

Whose house has the fewest people in it? _____

Each box of crayons has two reds, one orange, one yellow,
one green, one blue, one purple, two browns, and three blacks.
There are ten children in the class. Each has one box of crayons.

How many red crayons are there? _____

How many yellow crayons are there? _____

How many black crayons are there? _____

I live on Main Street. Keiko lives on North Street. Cristina lives on East Street. There are three white houses, four blue houses, and two red houses on my street. There are four white houses, five blue houses, three yellow houses, and one red house on Keiko's street. There are two red houses, two green houses, four brown houses, one yellow house, and one blue house on Cristina's street.

Whose street has the most houses? _____

Whose street has the fewest houses? _____

How many more blue houses than green are there? _____

Mr. Romero and Mr. Jones went to an orchard to buy fruit trees. They came home with the same number of trees. Mr. Romero got five apple trees, three peach trees, and four plum trees. Mr. Jones got six apple trees and two peach trees. The rest of Mr. Jones's trees were pear trees.

How many pear trees did Mr. Jones buy? _____

How many trees beginning with the letter P were bought? _____

Write a story to go with this number sentence. Make a picture to match.
Then give the answer.

6 + _____ = 10

_____

_____

_____

_____

_____

_____

_____

Write a story to go with this number sentence. Make a picture to match.
Then give the answer.

_____ + 5 = 9

_____

_____

_____

_____

_____

_____

READ IT! DRAW IT! SOLVE IT! • GRADE 2

Write a story to go with this number sentence. Make a picture to match. Then give the answer.

$8 + 5 =$ _____

_____

_____

_____

_____

_____

_____

_____

Write a story to go with this number sentence. Make a picture to match.
Then give the answer.

12 − 9 = _____

_____

_____

_____

_____

_____

_____

_____

Write a story to go with this number sentence. Make a picture to match. Then give the answer.

$10 - $ _____ $= 3$

_____

_____

_____

_____

_____

_____

_____

Write a story to go with this number sentence. Make a picture to match.
Then give the answer.

_____ − 1 = 1

_____

_____

_____

_____

_____

_____

_____

READ IT! DRAW IT! SOLVE IT! • GRADE 2

(blank drawing box)

Four-year-olds and five-year-olds are riding tricycles.
Six-year-olds and seven-year-olds are riding bicycles.
Franklin, Alicia, and Helen are four years old.
Shey, Amira, and Mary are five.
Nancy and Kim are six, and the triplets are seven.

Do we see more bicycles or tricycles? _____

How many wheels do we see? _____

Four cowboys each roped five bulls.

How many bulls were roped? _____

How many horns do we see? _____

[blank box for drawing]

There are nine players on a baseball team. The red team has six players. The blue team has seven players.

How many more players do we need? _____

I must buy gloves for all the players. How many will I need? _____

Draw different kinds of toys using each of these shapes:

square

circle

rectangle

triangle

Katerina grows fruit trees in her orchard. She planted
ten of each kind. She has plum trees, apple trees,
pear trees, peach trees, and cherry trees.

How many trees are in her orchard? _____

Five cherry trees blew down. Now how many trees

does she have? _____

[blank drawing box]

Eight sharks are swimming in the sea. Each one has
ten enormous teeth.

How many teeth do we see? _____

One shark loses four teeth. Now how many teeth do we see? _____

Aunt Martha has two sons and three daughters.
Uncle Paul has three sons and one daughter.
Uncle James has four sons.

How many cousins do I have? _____

Are there more boys or girls? _____

Each plant has two red tomatoes, three green tomatoes, and four yellow tomatoes. There are five plants.

How many tomatoes are there? _____

How many more yellow tomatoes than green? _____

How many more yellow tomatoes than red? _____

(blank box)

The parking lot holds 10 cars in each section.
There are 8 sections.

How many cars can the parking lot hold? _____

There are 58 cars in the lot now. How many empty

spaces are there? _____

When 10 more cars come, how many empty spaces

will there be? _____

Each helicopter has 4 blades. We see 36 blades.

How many helicopters are there? _____

If 2 helicopters take off, how many blades will we see? _____

(empty drawing box)

Ants have six legs. Spiders have eight legs.
Draw a picture of two ants, two spiders, two tigers, and two people.

How many legs do we see? _____

How many tails? _____

Three people play trumpets. Twice as many people play drums.

How many people in all? _____

Make pictures of animals using as many of these shapes as you can.

squares

circles

rectangles

triangles

Write a story to go with this number sentence. Make a picture to match.
Then give the answer.

20 + 30 = _____

_____

_____

_____

_____

_____

_____

There are ten animals in the zoo. Three are zebras,
two are monkeys, two are lions, and the rest are tigers.

How many tigers are there? _____

How many more zebras than monkeys? _____

How many fewer lions than zebras? _____

Write a story to go with this number sentence. Make a picture to match. Then give the answer.

_____ + 40 = 50

_____

_____

_____

_____

_____

_____

_____

Write a story to go with this number sentence. Make a picture to match.
Then give the answer.

60 − 30 = _____

_____

_____

_____

_____

_____

_____

_____

Write a story to go with this number sentence. Make a picture to match.
Then give the answer.

80 – _____ = 70

_____

_____

_____

_____

_____

_____

[blank drawing box]

Write a story to go with this number sentence. Make a picture to match.
Then give the answer.

_____ − 30 = 10

_____

_____

_____

_____

_____

_____

_____

We are going to decorate eggs. Ming has brought three
dozen eggs, Walter has brought five dozen, and Luis
has brought six dozen.

How many eggs did Luis bring? _____

How many eggs do we have in all? _____

The triplets are having a big birthday party. Each one has a cake.
It is their seventh birthday.

How many candles? _____

Each of the triplets has invited five friends.

How many people are at the party? _____

_____

We have an enormous birdbath. I see seven blue birds,
eight red birds, five yellow birds, and ten brown birds.

How many birds in all? _____

How many yellow and brown birds? _____

Marbles are five cents each. Stickers are a penny apiece.
I bought five marbles and three stickers. Abdul bought
seven marbles and six stickers.

How much money did I spend? _____

How much money did Abdul spend? _____

How much money did we both spend? _____

(blank drawing box)

We are at the circus. Three clowns ride each elephant.
There are eight elephants.

How many clowns? _____

How many tusks? _____

How many legs? _____

Make a picture of four things you could measure with your feet.

About how many feet long would each one be?

_____

_____

_____

_____

Draw five things that are taller than you are.

Then draw five things that are shorter than you are.

Draw five animals that are heavier than a cat.

Then draw five animals that are lighter than a cat.

Draw five things that can hold more milk than a drinking glass.

Then draw five things that hold less milk than a drinking glass.

Draw five things that are longer than a ruler.

Then draw five things that are shorter than a ruler.

Make a picture of five containers: one red, one orange,
one yellow, one green, and one blue. Draw them so that
the green one holds the most, the orange one holds the
least, and the red one holds twice as much as the orange
one and half as much as the green one.

Draw a brick. Draw five things that are heavier than a brick.

Then draw five things that are lighter than a brick.

[ ]

Draw five things you would measure using a ruler.

Then draw five things you would measure using a scale.

[ ]

Make pictures of six things that can hold water.
Color the ones that are bigger than a gallon blue.
Color the ones that are smaller than a gallon red.

(blank drawing box)

Make a picture of a bed.

How many people can sit on it? _____

How many elephants? _____

How many mice? _____

How many lions? _____

[blank work box]

We are building a wall with blocks. My wall is two blocks high and seven blocks long. May's wall is three blocks high and two blocks long. Aisha's wall is four blocks high and three blocks long.

Whose wall has used the most blocks? _____

Whose wall is the tallest? _____

Whose wall is the shortest? _____

Whose wall is the longest? _____

The big school bus holds 100 children. The minivans each hold 10 children. The big bus broke down with 48 children on it.

How many minivans will we need to get the children home? _____

How many extra seats will there be? _____

Name _____

The big school bus holds 100 children. The minivans
each hold 10 children. There are 5 full minivans—
2 with 3 empty seats, and 1 with 5 empty seats. All
these children get off the minivans and get onto the big bus.

How many empty seats will there be on the big bus? _____

When 32 children get off the big bus,

how many empty seats will there be? _____

[blank box]

We have little red balloons and big blue ones.
The red ones cost I cent and the blue ones cost I0 cents.
I have 36 red balloons. I want to trade them for blue ones.

How many blue balloons can I get? _____

How many red ones will I still have? _____

Blue balloons cost 10 cents. Red balloons cost 1 cent.
Tim owes me 25 cents. He wants to pay me in balloons.
He has only 3 blue balloons.

How can he do it? _____

_____

_____

What will he have left? _____

Blue balloons cost ten cents and red balloons cost one cent.
Jamaal has six red balloons and four blue balloons.
I have seven red balloons and three blue balloons.

How many of each color do we have?

blue _____

red _____

We trade them in so that we will have as many blue balloons as possible.
How many of each color will we have now?

blue _____

red _____

How much money are they worth? _____

Blue pinwheels cost 10 cents, green pinwheels cost
5 cents, and red pinwheels cost 1 cent. I want to have
as many of each color as I can. I have 47 cents.
How many of each color might I get?

red _____

green _____

blue _____

Blue balloons are worth ten cents. Red balloons are worth one cent. Pablo has five blue balloons and one red one. I have three blue balloons and four red ones.

What can I do to get a balloon collection that is worth the same as Pablo's?

_____

_____

_____

Blue balloons are worth ten cents. Red balloons are worth one cent. Simon has one blue balloon and seven red balloons. Amal has two blue balloons and four red ones.

How many balloons do they have in all?

blue _____

red _____

If they trade in the reds for a blue, how many will they have?

blue _____

red _____

Red beads are worth 1 cent. Blue beads are worth 10 cents. Yellow beads are worth 100 cents. I had 9 red beads, 3 blue beads, and 2 yellow beads. I got 3 red beads, 8 blue beads, and 4 yellow beads.

How many of each do I have?

red _____

blue _____

yellow _____

If I trade in the reds for a blue, how many of each will I have?

red _____

blue _____

yellow _____

Red beads are worth 1 cent. Blue beads are worth 10
cents. Yellow beads are worth 100 cents. I have
1 yellow bead, 2 blue beads, and 3 red beads. I owe
Amani 4 blue and 5 red beads.

How can I pay him? _____

_____

_____

_____

Red beads are worth 1 cent. Blue beads are worth 10 cents. Yellow beads are worth 100 cents. Mary has 9 red beads, 4 blue beads, and 2 yellow beads. I have 8 red beads, 7 blue beads, and 3 yellow beads.

When we put them together, how many of each color will we have?

red _____

blue _____

yellow _____

When we trade reds for a blue, and blues for a yellow, how many will we have?

red _____

blue _____

yellow _____

Write a story to go with this number sentence. Make a picture to match.
Then give the answer.

24 + 37 = _____

_____

_____

_____

_____

_____

_____

_____

Write a story to go with this number sentence. Make a picture to match.
Then give the answer.

$49 + \underline{\hspace{1.5cm}} = 61$

_____

_____

_____

_____

_____

_____

READ IT! DRAW IT! SOLVE IT! • GRADE 2

Write a story to go with this number sentence. Make a picture to match. Then give the answer.

_____ + 25 = 40

_____

_____

_____

_____

_____

_____

Write a story to go with this number sentence. Make a picture to match.
Then give the answer.

41 – 18 = _____

_____

_____

_____

_____

_____

_____

Write a story to go with this number sentence. Make a picture to match. Then give the answer.

$23 - \underline{\hspace{1.5cm}} = 7$

Write a story to go with this number sentence. Make a picture to match.
Then give the answer.

_____ − 35 = 19

_____

_____

_____

_____

_____

_____

Each classroom gets four kickballs, three footballs,
one baseball, and two basketballs.

How many balls does each classroom get? _____

If five classes put their footballs together,

how many will they have? _____

If five classes put footballs and kickballs together,

how many more kickballs than footballs will there be? _____

Draw things that might be in a classroom that would have these shapes in them.

a cone

a sphere

a cube

a cylinder

Make pictures of an eagle, a robin, a rabbit, a parrot, and a penguin.

Which one doesn't belong? _____

Why? _____

_____

Make pictures of a globe, the sun, a basketball, a stop sign, and a clock.

Which one doesn't belong? _____

Why? _____

_____

Make pictures of a hawk, a helicopter, a truck, a jet, and an owl.

Which one doesn't belong? _____

Why? _____

_____

Divide the box in half. Draw pictures of the things in the list below.
Put the things together that belong together.

a worm
a pine tree
a tulip
a dinosaur
a hedge
a canary

Why do the things in each group belong together?

_____

_____

_____

Divide the box in half. Draw pictures of the things in the list below.
Put the things together that belong together.

a train
a wizard
a unicorn
a computer
a fairy godmother
Abraham Lincoln

Why do the things in each group belong together? _____

_____

_____

I have 2 quarters, 3 dimes, 4 nickels, and 2 pennies.

How much money do I have? _____

If I spend 27 cents, how much money will I have? _____

It takes 10 ants to carry each cookie to the anthill.

How many cookies can 30 ants carry if they all take 4 trips? _____

How many cookies can they carry if they all take 8 trips? _____

Five Eskimos can live in each igloo.

How many Eskimos can live in 20 igloos? _____

How many Eskimos can live in eight igloos? _____

Make a picture of real or imaginary animals standing
in a line. There are 7 animals. Starting with the second
animal, every other one has 4 feet. The rest have 2 feet.

How many feet? _____

Nine children stand in line at the drinking fountain.
The odd ones are boys. The even ones are girls.

Are there more boys or girls? _____

Oranges cost 17 cents. Bananas cost 20 cents.
Cherries cost 3 cents. Apples cost 8 cents.
I have 3 quarters and 6 pennies.

What can I buy? _____

_____

_____

_____

_____

There are four panes in each window. My house has eight windows.

How many panes? _____

His house has seven windows.

How many panes? _____

How many more panes in my house than his? _____

READ IT! DRAW IT! SOLVE IT! • GRADE 2

[blank box for drawing]

Jessica raises dogs. Her poodle had four puppies, her German shepherd had five puppies, her Dalmatian had three puppies, and her bloodhound had six puppies.

How many dogs are there at Jessica's place? _____

She has found homes for eight puppies.

How many puppies still need homes? _____

[blank box]

Six children are wearing in-line skates. Each skate has five wheels.

How many legs do we see? _____

How many wheels do we see? _____

```
┌─────────────────────────────────────────────────┐
│                                                   │
│                                                   │
│                                                   │
│                                                   │
│                                                   │
│                                                   │
│                                                   │
│                                                   │
│                                                   │
│                                                   │
│                                                   │
└─────────────────────────────────────────────────┘
```

Sam made a design with stars. Seven of the stars
have six points each. Six of the stars have five points.
Five of the stars have three points.

How many points? _____

How many more six-pointed stars

than three-pointed stars are there? _____

Make a picture of a window box with four flowers in it.
If we had five window boxes with the same number
of flowers in each, how many flowers would we

have? _____

If each box were twice the size, how many

flowers could each one hold? _____

Then how many flowers would we have in all? _____

1.

2.

3.

4.

Make four different pictures of your bedroom.
Put a clock on the wall in each picture.
Have the clock in each picture show what time
it might be when you are:

1. getting up

2. going to school

3. coming home from school

4. going to bed

1.	2.
3.	4.

Make four different pictures of the classroom with a clock on the wall in each picture. Have the clock show what time it is when you are:

1. starting school

2. having recess

3. going to lunch

4. getting ready to go home

```



```

The top shelf of the bookcase holds 24 books.
The second shelf holds 35 books. The bottom shelf
holds 48 books.

How many books are in the bookcase? _____

If we took 10 books from the shelves,

how many books would be left? _____

Draw these people:

Kito is 30 years old.

José is 1 year old.

Lana is 80 years old.

Mandy is 12 years old.

Draw these people, using yesterday's drawing as a guide.

Jared is 40 years older than Kito.

Betsy is 8 months younger than José.

Chin is 30 years older than Mandy.

Susan is 6 years younger than Mandy.

Here is a set of quintuplets riding tricycles.

How many fingers? _____

How many eyes? _____

How many wheels? _____

We took a vote to see which colors people liked the most.
Ten people liked red best. Eight people liked green best.
Nine people liked blue best. Seven people liked yellow best.

Use a ruler and draw a chart to show this.

How many people voted? _____

A bushel basket holds 20 apples. We came home with 4 full baskets.

How many apples did we pick? _____

If we had picked 95 apples, how many

baskets would we need? _____

Draw a chart to show the number of pets at our pet show.
We had five kittens, three turtles, and seven dogs.

How many more dogs than kittens? _____

How many fewer turtles than dogs? _____

We are having a sailboat race. Each boat has two red sails and three yellow ones. There are seven boats.

How many red sails? _____

How many yellow sails? _____

How many sails in all? _____

People are racing in long boats. There are six people
rowing in each boat. There are four boats racing.
Each person has two oars.

How many people? _____

How many oars? _____

We are having a relay race. There are eight people on each team.
There are six teams.

How many people? _____

If you divide each team in half, how many people

would there be? _____

Use four rectangles, two squares, five circles, and three triangles to make a design.

Draw a big rectangle. Divide it into sixths.

Color $\frac{1}{6}$ red, $\frac{2}{6}$ yellow, and $\frac{3}{6}$ blue.

There are 21 people in our class. We divided the class into thirds.
$\frac{1}{3}$ are in the red group, $\frac{1}{3}$ are in the yellow group,
and $\frac{1}{3}$ are in the blue group.

How many are in the yellow group? _____

How many altogether are in the red and blue groups? _____

We ordered a large pizza divided into quarters. $\frac{1}{4}$ has green peppers, $\frac{1}{4}$ has only cheese, and $\frac{2}{4}$ have meatballs.

Make a picture of the pizza.

Draw a clock. Place the hands to show that the time is 2:30.

Divide the clock into quarters.

In the first quarter you see the numbers 1, 2, and 3.

What numbers appear in each of the other quarters?

_____

_____

_____

We divided our garden into thirds. There are the same
number of plants in each section. In $\frac{1}{3}$ we planted tomatoes.
In $\frac{1}{3}$ we planted green peppers. In $\frac{1}{3}$ we planted corn.
We have 24 plants in all.

How many plants are in each section? _____

How many tomato and pepper plants together? _____

Mr. Brown divided his herd into thirds. He has 27 cows. $\frac{1}{3}$ of the cows are brown. $\frac{1}{3}$ of the cows are black. $\frac{1}{3}$ of the cows are red.

How many red cows are there? _____

How many black and brown cows together? _____

It takes five balloons to lift one elf into the air. Nine elves are flying.

How many balloons? _____

How many more balloons would we need

to get two more elves into the air? _____

Make a group of 16 houses.

Color $\frac{1}{4}$ of the houses red,

$\frac{1}{4}$ blue, $\frac{1}{4}$ green, and $\frac{1}{4}$ brown.

Make a group of 18 blocks. Color $\frac{1}{6}$ of the blocks red. Color $\frac{1}{6}$ of them blue.

How many blocks in $\frac{2}{6}$? _____

How many blocks in $\frac{3}{6}$? _____

How many blocks in $\frac{4}{6}$? _____

How many blocks in $\frac{5}{6}$? _____

READ IT! DRAW IT! SOLVE IT! • GRADE 2

Four girls lead the parade. Each girl holds two flags in each hand.

How many flags? _____

Color $\frac{1}{2}$ of the flags yellow and $\frac{1}{2}$ of them blue.

In the circus there are two clowns. There are twice as many elephants as clowns. There are twice as many lions as elephants. There are two more bears than lions. There are half as many ponies as bears.

How many elephants? _____

How many bears? _____

How many ponies? _____

In our garden we have five tulips. We have four times as many daisies as tulips. We have half as many daffodils as daisies.

How many daisies? _____

How many daffodils? _____

There are 20 cars for sale. $\frac{1}{2}$ of the cars are red.
$\frac{1}{4}$ of the cars are yellow. The rest are green.

How many cars are green? _____

How many cars are red? _____

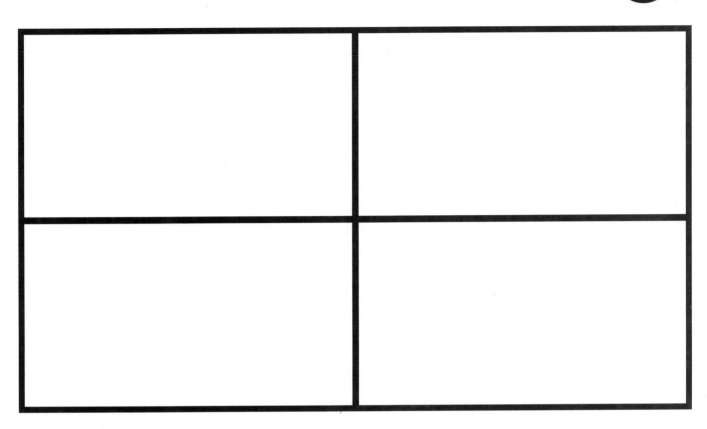

There are 12 months in the year. The year is divided into quarters.

How many months are in each quarter? _____

Give a name to each quarter, and draw a picture of something that might happen in that season.

A week is divided into seven days.

Give a name to each day.

Make a picture of yourself on each of the days.

We have 100 sandwiches to pass out to the people in our class.

How many sandwiches would each person
get if there were 10 people in the class? _____

How many sandwiches would each person
get if there were 20 people in the class? _____

John is two feet tall. Sam is twice as tall as John.
Their father is three times as tall as John.

How tall is Sam? _____

How tall is their father? _____

[blank drawing box]

The plum tree has 8 plums. The peach tree has 10 peaches. The apple tree has 12 apples. Two of us are picking the fruit. We will each get the same number of each kind of fruit.

How much will we each get?

peaches _____

apples _____

plums _____

Insects have six legs.

How many shoes must we get for ten ants? _____

How many shoes must we get for seven bees? _____

Eight fish swim in each tank. There are seven tanks.

How many fish? _____

Half of the fish in each tank are red, and half are yellow.

How many yellow fish in one tank? _____

How many red fish in all? _____

It is two miles from my house to Makoto's. It is twice
as far from Makoto's house to Ben's.

How far is it from my house to Ben's? _____

We can buy a baseball card for one cent. A marble costs ten cents. Tom has lots of baseball cards but not enough marbles. He trades with Bill and gets two marbles.

How many baseball cards did he give to Bill? _____

What might happen if he gave Bill 48 baseball cards? _____

_____

_____

_____

Draw the American flag as it would look if there were 20 states.

Draw a 100-yard football field and label every tenth yard line.

A big puzzle is on the table. Five of us sit on wooden
chairs working on the puzzle.

How many wooden legs? _____

How many legs in all? _____

This tree has ten branches. There are five twigs on the end of each branch.

How many twigs? _____

There are three leaves on each twig.

How many leaves? _____

This train has 50 cars. The first ten cars are red.
The next ten are orange. The next ten are yellow.
The next ten are green. The last ten are blue.

What color is car #23? _____

What color is car #18? _____

What color is car #48? _____

The roof of this building is on fire. Firefighters are going up the ladder to put the fire out. Joe is on the 46th rung. Tanya is five rungs lower than Joe. Maria is on the 26th rung. Kesia is seven rungs higher than Maria.

What rung is Tanya on? _____

What rung is Kesia on? _____

Draw a design with one circle, one square, one rectangle, and one triangle. Make the design symmetrical.

There are 10 crayons in a box. One table has 4 full boxes of crayons and 8 extra crayons. The other table has 5 full boxes and 9 extra crayons.

How many crayons in all? _____

There are 10 crayons in each box. We had 5 full boxes and 2 extra crayons. We gave away 38 crayons.

How many crayons are left? _____